Why Wyoming?

BY

ROBIN GAIL BUNN

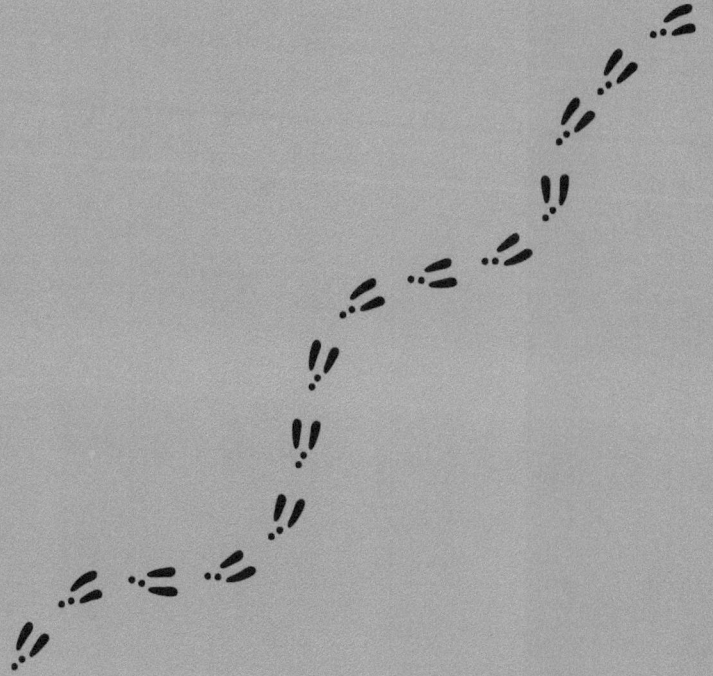

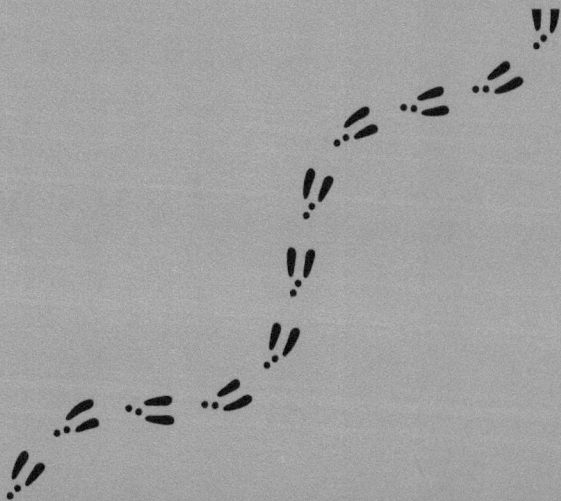

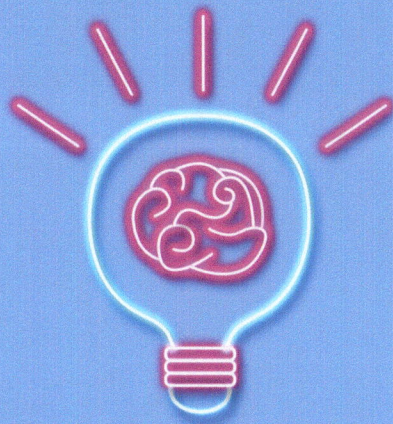

TO ALL THE CHILDREN WHO LIVE IN WYOMING—AND ALL THE CHILDREN WHO DON'T.

WHY WYOMING? WHY LIVE HERE?
THE ANSWER'S REALLY CRYSTAL CLEAR!

WIDE OPEN SPACES, SKIES SO BLUE,
MOUNTAINS, PRAIRIES, AND RIVERS, TOO.

ON THE WESTERN SIDE OF THE USA, YOU'LL FIND WYOMING TUCKED AWAY.

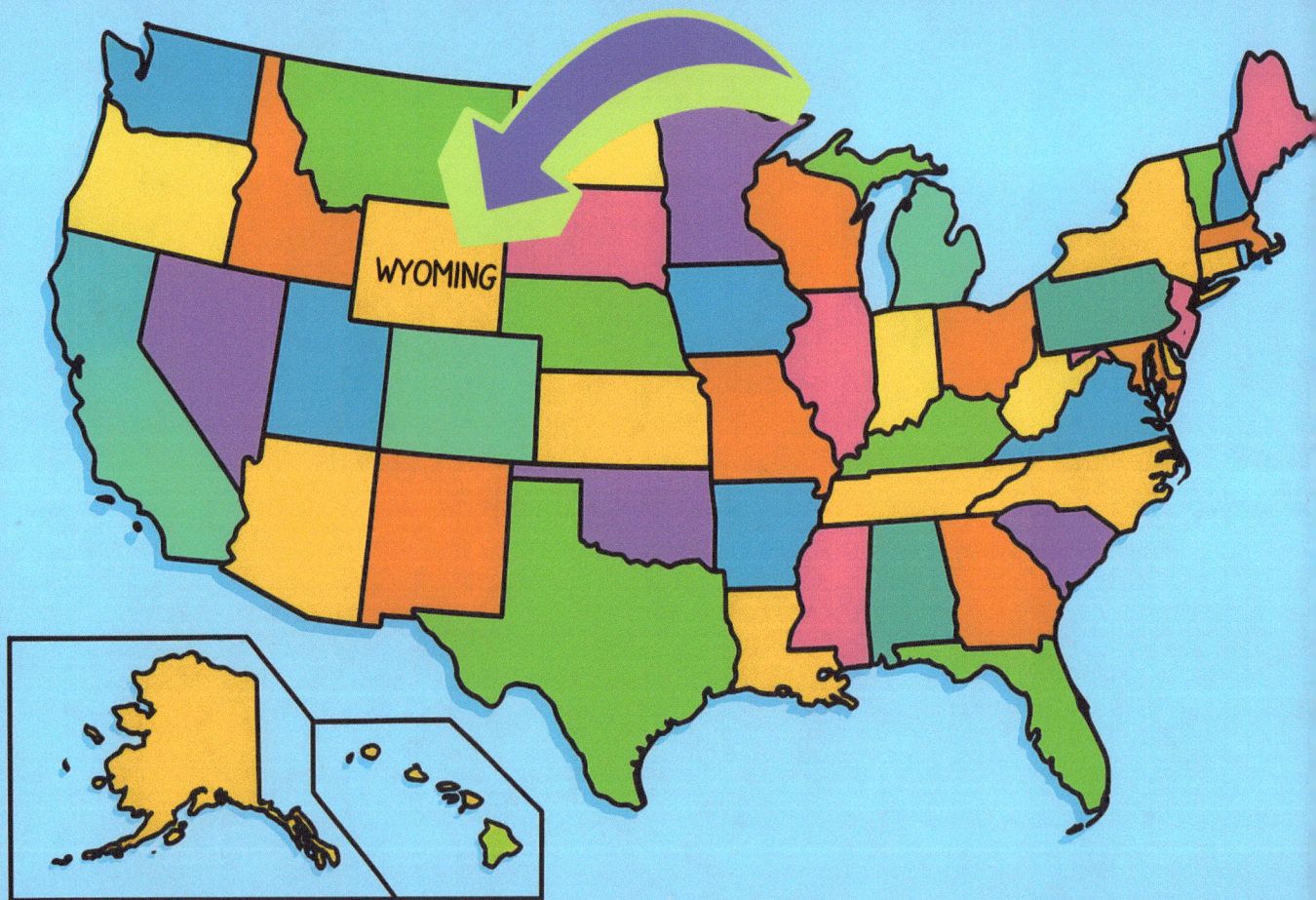

SEE THESE FUN PLACES ON THE MAP? READ ON FOR SOME FUN AND QUIRKY FACTS!

BEAR TOOTH HIGHWAY

SHERIDAN

OLD FAITHFUL

BUFFALO

DEVILS TOWER

BIG HORN MTNS

GILLETTE

JACKSON

THERMOPOLIS

GRAND TETONS

WIND RIVER RANGE

CASPER

DOUGLAS

WYOMING RANGE

GREEN RIVER FOSSIL SITE

ROCK SPRINGS

LARAMIE

CHEYENNE

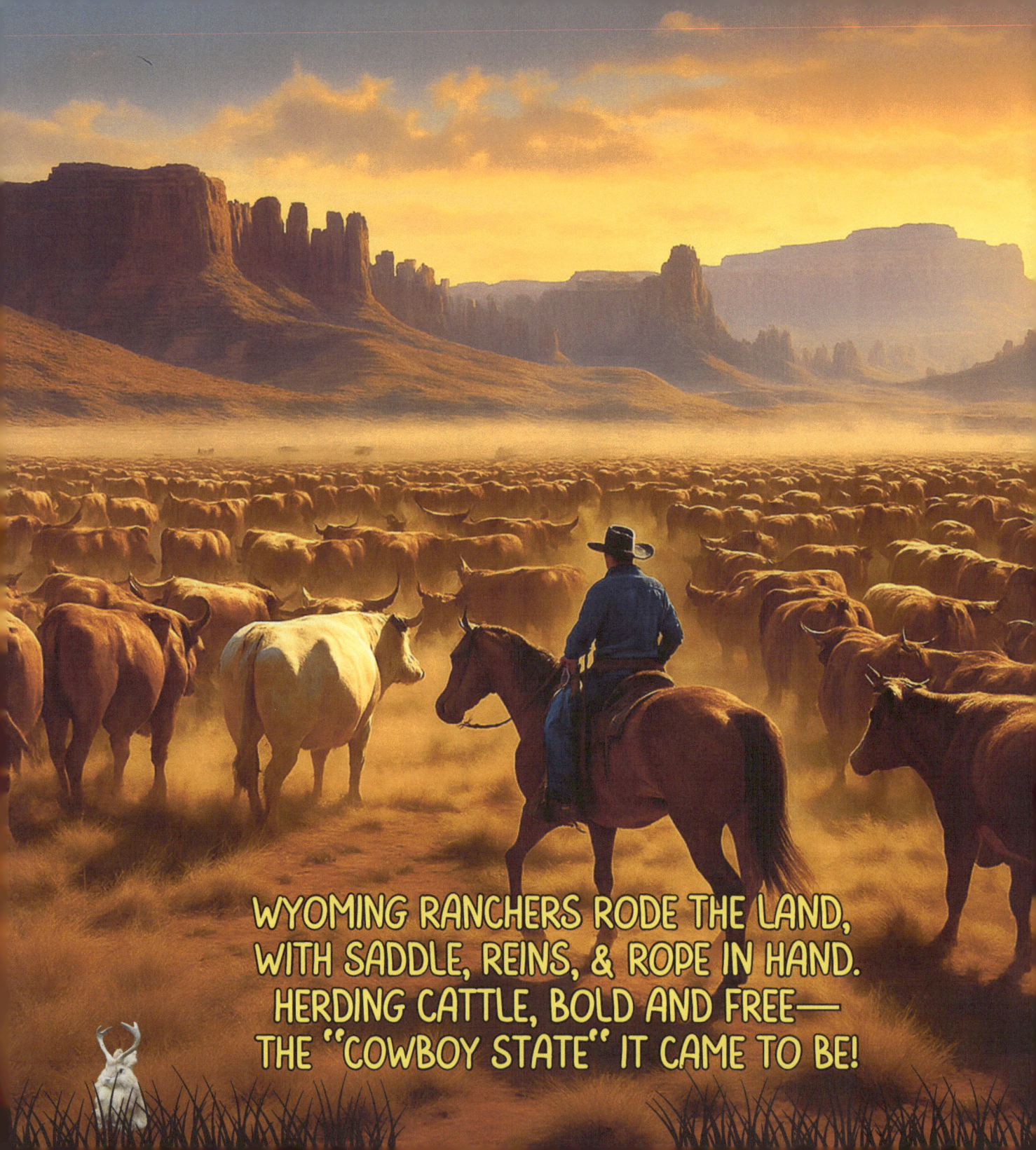

WYOMING RANCHERS RODE THE LAND,
WITH SADDLE, REINS, & ROPE IN HAND.
HERDING CATTLE, BOLD AND FREE—
THE "COWBOY STATE" IT CAME TO BE!

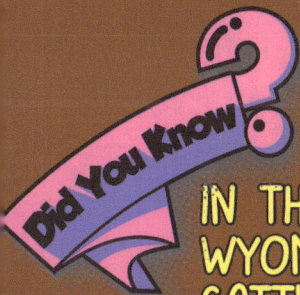

IN THE LATE 1800S, CATTLE RANCHING WAS THE HEART OF WYOMING LIFE. COWBOYS RODE THE WIDE PRAIRIES, MOVING CATTLE ON LONG DRIVES AND CARING FOR BIG RANCHES. THEIR BRAVERY, GRIT, AND INDEPENDENCE HELPED SHAPE THE STATE.

TODAY, THE COWBOY SPIRIT IS EVERYWHERE! YOU'LL SPOT WYOMING'S FAMOUS BUCKING HORSE AND RIDER ON LICENSE PLATES AND EVEN CHEERING ON THE UNIVERSITY OF WYOMING. THE "CODE OF THE WEST" REMINDS PEOPLE TO LEND A HAND, GREET OTHERS WITH A SMILE, AND TAKE CARE OF THE LAND.

AND HERE'S THE BEST PART: IN WYOMING, ANYONE CAN BE A COWBOY—NO MATTER YOUR AGE OR GENDER—SO LONG AS YOU LIVE WITH COURAGE, KINDNESS, AND RESPECT FOR NATURE. THAT'S WHY WYOMING IS CALLED THE COWBOY STATE!

OLD FAITHFUL GEYSER MAKES YELLOWSTONE PROUD,
IT BLASTS WITH A WHOOSH AS CROWDS CHEER LOUD.
STEAM AND HOT WATER SPRAY UP SO HIGH,
IT'S NATURE'S OWN FOUNTAIN BENEATH THE BLUE SKY.

YELLOWSTONE HAS MORE THAN 500 GEYSERS—THAT'S OVER HALF OF ALL THE GEYSERS ON EARTH! THE MOST FAMOUS ONE IS OLD FAITHFUL, WHICH SHOOTS HOT WATER UP TO 180 FEET HIGH ABOUT EVERY 90 MINUTES.

THE WORD "GEYSER" COMES FROM ICELAND. IN THE 1700S, PEOPLE THERE NAMED A POWERFUL HOT SPRING "GEYSIR," WHICH MEANS "TO GUSH." THE NAME STUCK, AND NOW WE USE "GEYSER" FOR ALL HOT SPRINGS THAT BLAST WATER AND STEAM INTO THE AIR.

VIÐ SKULUM KALLA ÞAÐ „GEYSIR"

DEVILS TOWER IS MADE OF ROCK,
RISING HIGH, IT'S QUITE A SHOCK!
SCRATCHES DOWN ITS SIDES YOU'LL SEE—
WHO MADE THOSE MARKS? A BEAR, MAYBE!!

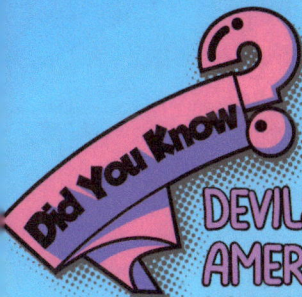

DEVILS TOWER WAS NAMED AMERICA'S VERY FIRST NATIONAL MONUMENT IN 1906 BY PRESIDENT THEODORE ROOSEVELT. IT'S ONE OF THE MOST FAMOUS LANDMARKS IN WYOMING!

SOME NATIVE AMERICAN TRIBES TELL THE STORY OF TWO BOYS BEING CHASED BY A GIANT BEAR. THE BOYS PRAYED TO THE GREAT SPIRIT TO SAVE THEM. SUDDENLY THE GROUND THEY WERE STANDING ON ROSE UP, CREATING A TOWER. WHEN THE BEAR TRIED TO CLIMB THE TOWER, ITS CLAWS SCRATCHED THE SIDES, LEAVING THE DEEP GROOVES WE SEE TODAY.

HERE IN THERMOPOLIS, WATER FLOWS,
HEATED BY MAGMA FROM FAR BELOW.
POOLS SO WARM, WITH COLORS BRIGHT,
A NATURAL WONDER AND PURE DELIGHT!

BIG SPRING IN THERMOPOLIS IS ONE OF THE LARGEST MINERAL HOT SPRINGS IN THE WORLD! THE WATER BURSTS FROM THE GROUND AT A STEAMY 135°F (57°C) AND FLOWS ACROSS COLORFUL TERRACES, COOLING NATURALLY AS IT TRAVELS. BY THE TIME IT REACHES THE STATE BATH HOUSE, IT'S ABOUT 104°F (40°C)—WHICH IS STILL PRETTY HOT FOR A BATH!

MAYBE WE SHOULD ASK THE PARK RANGERS TO DUMP IN A FEW BAGS OF ICE CUBES TO COOL IT DOWN!

ICE

ICE

THERMOPOLIS IS ALSO THE PLACE TO GO
FOR DINOSAUR BONES FROM LONG AGO.
BURIED DEEP, BUT NOW ARE FOUND,
AMAZING FOSSILS IN THE GROUND!

THERMOPOLIS IS HOME TO THE WYOMING DINOSAUR CENTER, ONE OF THE LARGEST FOSSIL MUSEUMS IN THE WORLD. ITS STAR IS "JIMBO," A SUPERSAURUS THAT STRETCHED OVER 100 FEET LONG—LONGER THAN THREE SCHOOL BUSES!

KIDS CAN EVEN SIGN UP TO BE JUNIOR PALEONTOLOGISTS FOR A DAY. A PALEONTOLOGIST IS A SCIENTIST WHO STUDIES FOSSILS, LIKE DINOSAUR BONES, TO LEARN ABOUT LIFE MILLIONS OF YEARS AGO. AT THERMOPOLIS, KIDS GET TO DIG, BRUSH, AND HELP UNCOVER REAL FOSSILS!

DRUMS KEEP RHYTHM AS DANCERS SWAY,
STORIES TOLD IN A SACRED WAY.
AT POWWOWS, PAST AND PRESENT MEET,
TRADITIONS ARE HONORED, AND PROUD HEARTS BEAT.

POWWOWS ON THE WIND RIVER RESERVATION BRING PEOPLE TOGETHER TO CELEBRATE AMERICAN INDIAN CULTURE AND HISTORY. DANCERS WEAR TRADITIONAL REGALIA DECORATED WITH BEADS, FEATHERS, AND OTHER DECORATIONS, WHILE DRUMMERS AND SINGERS SHARE SONGS PASSED DOWN THROUGH GENERATIONS.

THESE GATHERINGS CONNECT FAMILIES AND FRIENDS, AND KEEP TRADITIONS ALIVE FOR THE FUTURE—SHOWING HOW HISTORY AND PRIDE STILL BEAT IN EVERY HEART.

HIGH ABOVE THE LAND THEY SOAR,
BALD EAGLES SPREAD THEIR WINGS ONCE MORE.
WITH KEEN EYES SHINING, SHARP AND BRIGHT,
THEY RULE THE SKIES IN GRACEFUL FLIGHT.

WYOMING IS HOME TO ONE OF THE HIGHEST CONCENTRATIONS OF BALD EAGLES IN THE ROCKY MOUNTAIN REGION, ESPECIALLY IN WINTER WHEN MANY MIGRATE SOUTH TO HUNT ALONG THE STATE'S RIVERS AND LAKES. THESE POWERFUL BIRDS CAN GROW WINGSPANS OF UP TO 7 FEET ACROSS—AS WIDE AS A CAR! THEIR GIANT NESTS CAN GROW AS WIDE AS A DINING TABLE AND WEIGH OVER A THOUSAND POUNDS AFTER YEARS OF REBUILDING.

A BALD EAGLE'S EYESIGHT IS ABOUT FOUR TIMES SHARPER THAN OURS—THEY CAN SPOT A RABBIT OR FISH FROM NEARLY TWO MILES AWAY!

IN WYOMING, LEGENDS HOP AND PLAY,
A RABBIT WITH HORNS MIGHT PASS YOUR WAY!
SOME SAY IT SINGS A COWBOY TUNE—
OUT ON THE PRAIRIE BENEATH THE MOON.

THE JACKALOPE LEGEND STARTED IN DOUGLAS, WYOMING IN THE 1930S! TWO BROTHERS PUT ANTELOPE HORNS ON A STUFFED RABBIT AS A JOKE. PEOPLE LOVED IT SO MUCH THAT DOUGLAS BECAME THE "HOME OF THE JACKALOPE."

THE CRITTER HAS BECOME SO FAMOUS IN WYOMING THAT TOWNS LIKE DOUGLAS HAND OUT "JACKALOPE HUNTING LICENSES." THE LICENSE SAYS YOU CAN ONLY HUNT THE JACKALOPE ON JUNE 31ST (A DAY THAT DOESN'T EXIST!) AND YOU MUST WEAR A FRYING PAN ON YOUR HEAD TO PROTECT YOURSELF —BECAUSE JACKALOPES ARE SAID TO BE DANGEROUS WHEN STARTLED!

FOSSIL FISH, IN ROCKS WE SEE,
FROZEN IN STONE FROM AN ANCIENT SEA.
SCALES AND FINS STILL SHINING BRIGHT,
ALL FROM THE GREEN RIVER FOSSIL SITE.

THE GREEN RIVER FORMATION IN WYOMING IS ONE OF THE RICHEST FOSSIL BEDS IN THE WORLD. THE GREEN RIVER FORMATION ISN'T FROM TODAY'S GREEN RIVER— IT'S FROM ANCIENT LAKES THAT COVERED WYOMING ABOUT 50 MILLION YEARS AGO! WHEN THOSE LAKES EVENTUALLY DRIED UP, LAYERS OF MUD AND SEDIMENT TURNED INTO ROCK, PERFECTLY PRESERVING FISH, TURTLES, INSECTS, AND EVEN PLANTS AS FOSSILS. SOME SLABS LOOK LIKE A WHOLE SCHOOL OF FISH WAS FROZEN IN STONE!

50 MILLION YEARS AGO

TODAY

BUFFALO'S MAIN STREET IS OH SO LONG.
PAST SHOPS AND CAFES, IT ROLLS ALONG.
FROM END TO END, IT JUST WON'T QUIT—
A VERY LONG MAIN STREET. CAN YOU IMAGINE IT!?

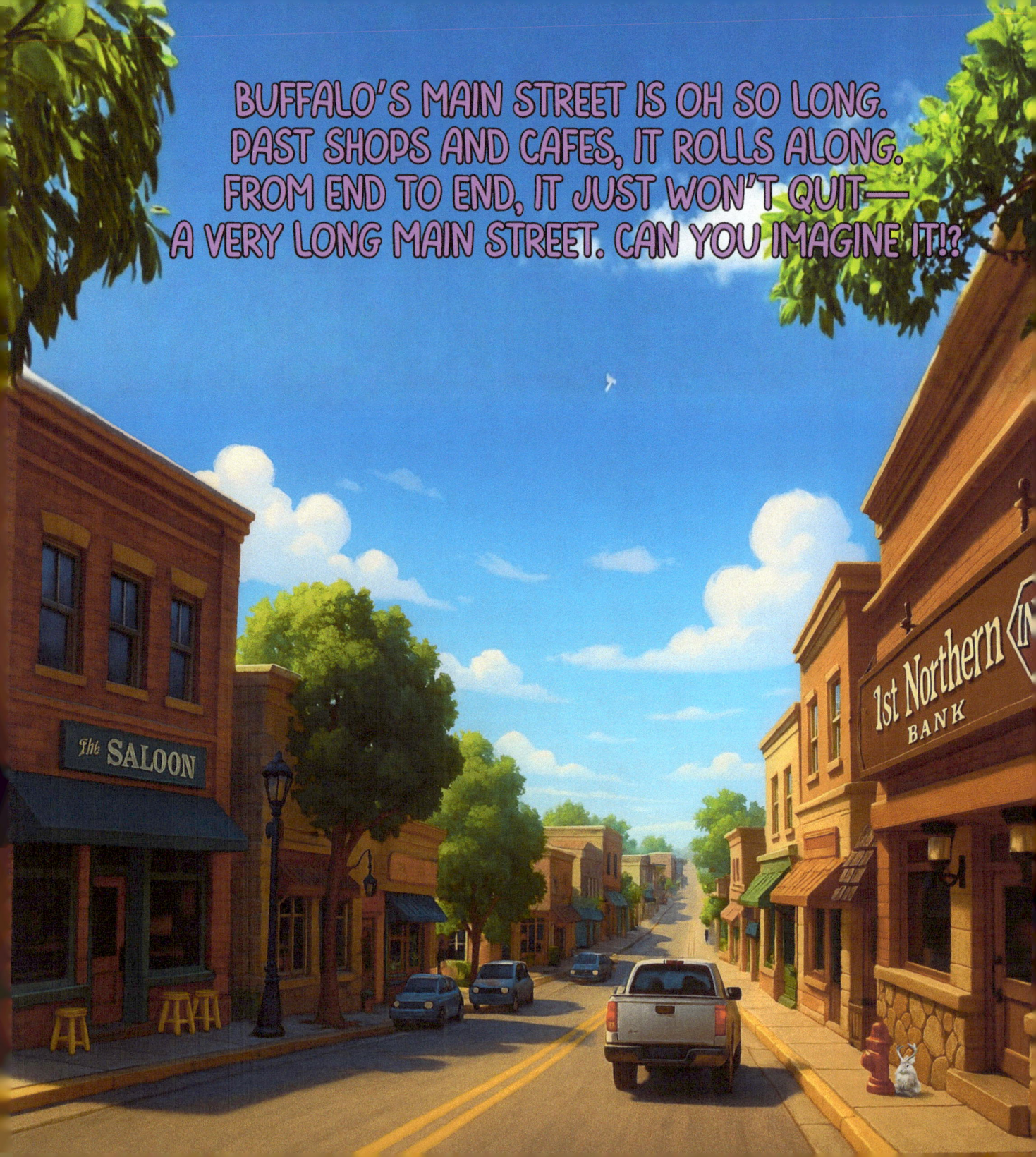

MAIN STREET IN THE TOWN OF BUFFALO, WYOMING, IS ACTUALLY HIGHWAY 16. THIS INDEPENDENT STRETCH OF HIGHWAY 16 STARTS IN BUFFALO AND ENDS IN WORLAND, WYOMING, WHICH MAKES THIS OLD WEST STREET FEEL EXTRA LONG. ALONG MAIN STREET, IN BUFFALO, YOU'LL FIND CHARMING SHOPS, CAFES, AND THE HISTORIC— AND SOME SAY HAUNTED—OCCIDENTAL HOTEL, WHERE FAMOUS OUTLAWS ONCE STAYED!

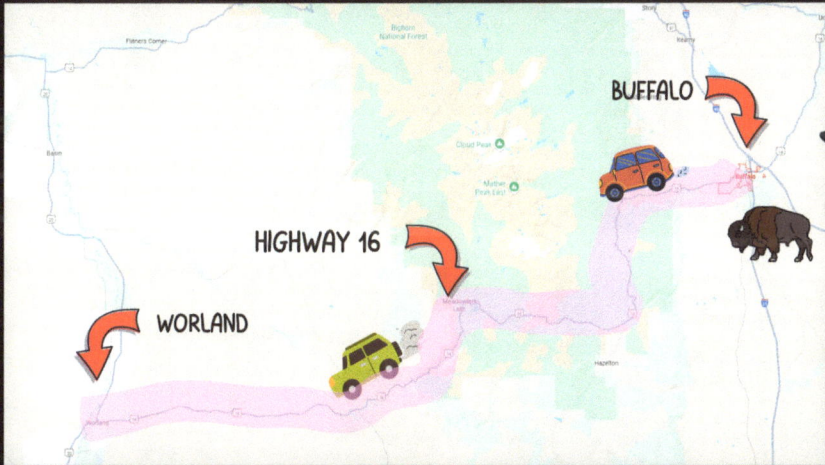

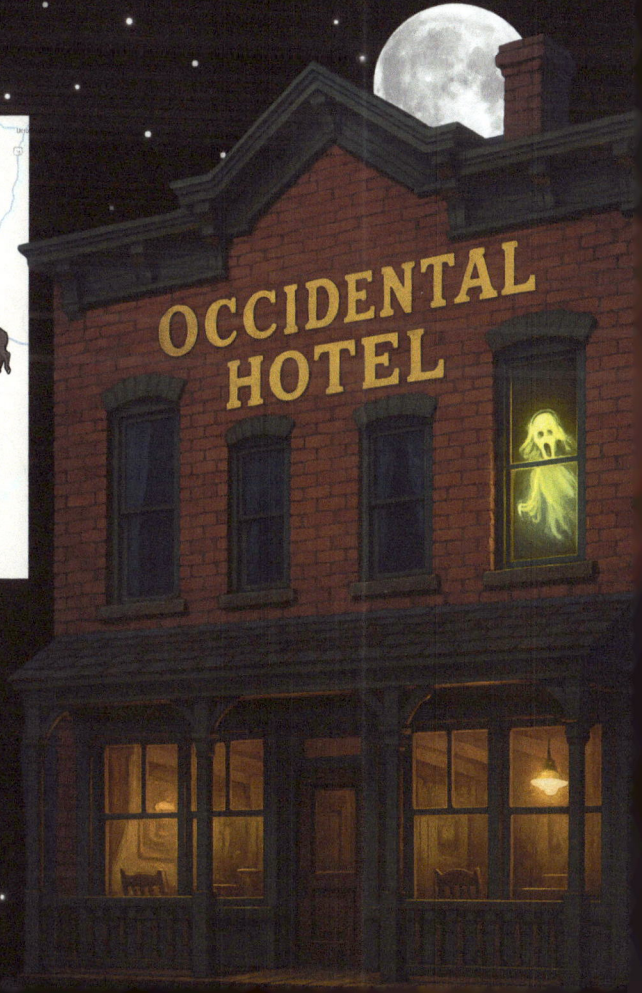

BUFFALO

HIGHWAY 16

WORLAND

OCCIDENTAL HOTEL

IN JACKSON, WHAT A SIGHT TO SEE,
AN ARCH OF ELK ANTLERS AS TALL AS A TREE.
CLOSE TO THE TETONS, PROUD AND TALL,
VISITORS COME TO SEE IT ALL.

THE TOWN SQUARE IN JACKSON HAS FOUR GIANT ARCHES MADE FROM THOUSANDS OF ELK ANTLERS! EVERY SPRING, LOCAL BOY SCOUTS COLLECT SHED ANTLERS FROM THE NEARBY NATIONAL ELK REFUGE TO HELP BUILD AND REPAIR THE ARCHES.

JACKSON IS JUST A SHORT DRIVE FROM GRAND TETON NATIONAL PARK, SO MANY VISITORS STOP TO SEE BOTH THE TOWERING MOUNTAINS AND THE FAMOUS ANTLER ARCHES ON THE SAME TRIP!

OLD GHOST TOWNS WHERE MINERS STAYED,
NOW STAND QUIET, THEIR MEMORIES FADE.
EMPTY STREETS AND DOORS THAT CREAK,
WHISPERS OF HISTORY PLAY HIDE-AND-SEEK.

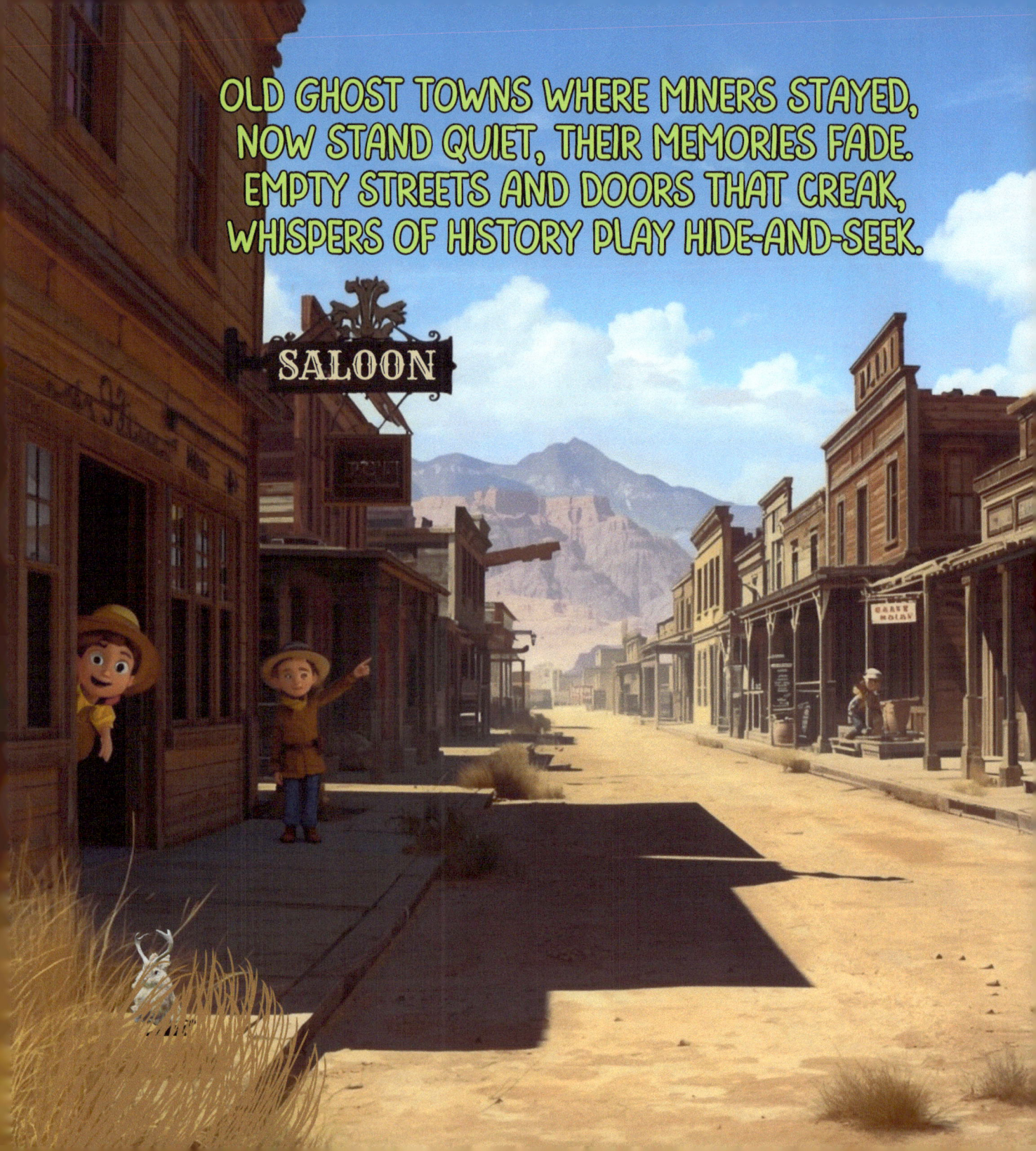

SALOON

WYOMING HAS OVER 100 GHOST TOWNS! THESE TOWNS WERE ONCE BUSY WITH MINERS, COWBOYS, AND RAILROAD WORKERS, BUT WHEN THE GOLD AND COAL RAN OUT, THE PEOPLE MOVED AWAY. ONE OF THE MOST FAMOUS, SOUTH PASS CITY, STILL STANDS TODAY WITH OLD WOODEN BUILDINGS YOU CAN EXPLORE—IT'S LIKE STEPPING BACK IN TIME!

NEAR ROCK SPRINGS, WHAT DO WE SEE?
MUSTANGS GALLOPING, WILD AND FREE.
BROUGHT BY SPANIARDS LONG AGO,
NOW IN WYOMING, THEY LIVE AND GROW.

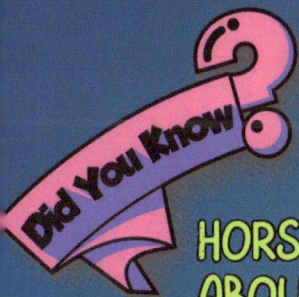

HORSES ONCE LIVED IN NORTH AMERICA BUT DISAPPEARED ABOUT 10,000 YEARS AGO. WHEN SPANISH EXPLORERS ARRIVED IN THE 1500S, THEY BROUGHT STRONG, FAST HORSES FROM SPAIN AND NORTH AFRICA—AND REINTRODUCED HORSES TO THIS LAND!

SOME OF THOSE HORSES ESCAPED OR WERE SET FREE AND LEARNED TO SURVIVE ON THEIR OWN. OVER TIME, THEIR DESCENDANTS BECAME THE WILD MUSTANGS THAT STILL ROAM WYOMING'S OPEN PLAINS TODAY.

IN CAMPBELL COUNTY, MINERS BLAST,
TO REACH THE COAL FROM AGES PAST.
TRUCKS AS TALL AS HOUSES ROLL,
AND MILE-LONG TRAINS HAUL WYOMING COAL!

WYOMING'S CAMPBELL COUNTY MAKES MORE COAL THAN ANY OTHER COUNTY IN THE UNITED STATES! NEAR GILLETTE, THE BLACK THUNDER AND NORTH ANTELOPE ROCHELLE MINES ARE SO BIG THAT THE COAL TRUCKS LOOK LIKE GIANTS— EACH ONE IS TALLER THAN A TWO-STORY HOUSE! THE COAL THEY HAUL RIDES AWAY ON TRAINS THAT CAN STRETCH OVER A MILE LONG! IT'S RICH COAL AND OIL RESESRVES IS WHY GILLETTE CALLS ITSELF THE ENERGY CAPITAL OF THE NATION.

WHERE WAGON TRAINS ONCE CROSSED THE PLAIN,
THROUGH WIND AND DUST AND SUN AND RAIN,
NOW DRILLING RIGS REACH DEEP BELOW—
FOR "BLACK GOLD" THAT HELPS WYOMING GROW!

CASPER EARNED ITS NICKNAME "THE OIL CITY" DURING WYOMING'S EARLY OIL BOOM! BUT LONG BEFORE THAT, IT WAS A STOP ON THE OREGON TRAIL, WHERE PIONEERS CROSSED THE NORTH PLATTE RIVER ON THEIR JOURNEY WEST.

NEAR THE TOWN OF GUERNSEY, YOU CAN STILL SEE DEEP WAGON RUTS CARVED INTO THE ROCK MORE THAN 150 YEARS AGO, AND AT CASPER'S NATIONAL HISTORIC TRAILS CENTER, YOU CAN WALK IN THE FOOTSTEPS OF REAL PIONEERS!

IN WYOMING'S PAST, A CHOICE WAS MADE,
FOR WOMEN'S VOICES TO BE WEIGHED.
THE FIRST TO VOTE, TO LEAD, TO STAND—
EQUALITY SHINES ACROSS THIS LAND.

WYOMING WAS THE FIRST PLACE IN THE UNITED STATES WHERE WOMEN COULD VOTE—WAY BACK IN 1869! THAT'S WHY IT'S CALLED THE EQUALITY STATE.

LATER, WYOMING MADE HISTORY WHEN NELLIE TAYLOE ROSS BECAME THE FIRST FEMALE GOVERNOR IN THE WHOLE COUNTRY IN 1925. THE GOVERNOR'S MANSION AND THE WYOMING STATE CAPITAL ARE LOCATED IN CHEYENNE.

GOVERNOR

OUR CAPITOL IN CHEYENNE STANDS PROUD AND TALL,
AND COWBOYS GATHER FOR THE "DADDY OF 'EM ALL!"
PARADES, BRONCOS, AND FIREWORKS FLY
AS FRONTIER DAYS LIGHT UP THE SKY!

CHEYENNE IS WYOMING'S CAPITAL CITY AND HOME TO CHEYENNE FRONTIER DAYS, THE LARGEST OUTDOOR RODEO IN THE WORLD! SINCE 1897, PEOPLE HAVE COME FROM ALL OVER TO CHEER, RIDE, AND CELEBRATE THE WILD WEST DURING THIS TEN DAY-LONG FESTIVAL OF COWBOY FUN. AT THE FREE PANCAKE BREAKFAST, LOCALS COOK UP OVER 100,000 FLAPJACKS, USING CEMENT MIXERS TO STIR THE BATTER. IMAGINE STACKING ALL THOSE PANCAKES—IT WOULD MAKE A TOWER TALLER THAN THE STATUE OF LIBERTY!

BUFFALO BILL CODY BUILT THIS TOWN,
WHERE RODEO RIDERS EARN THEIR CROWN.
THE RODEO CAPITAL OF THE WORLD, THEY SAY—
CODY STILL CHEERS THE COWBOY WAY!

THE TOWN OF CODY WAS FOUNDED BY BUFFALO BILL CODY, A FAMOUS SHOWMAN AND COWBOY WHO TRAVELED THE WORLD PERFORMING IN HIS "WILD WEST SHOW." TODAY, CODY PROUDLY CALLS ITSELF THE RODEO CAPITAL OF THE WORLD! THE CODY NITE RODEO HAS BEEN HELD EVERY SUMMER NIGHT SINCE 1938, MAKING IT ONE OF THE LONGEST-RUNNING RODEOS IN THE COUNTRY.

IN SHERIDAN, WYOMING, WHERE COWBOYS STAY,
THE SHERIDAN INN STILL LIGHTS THE WAY.
NAMED AFTER A GENERAL, PROUD AND TRUE,
IT'S WHERE HOT TAMALE LOUIE FED FOLKS, TOO!

SHERIDAN WAS NAMED AFTER GENERAL PHILIP SHERIDAN, A FAMOUS CIVIL WAR HERO. THE HISTORIC SHERIDAN INN, BUILT IN 1893, WAS ONE OF THE FIRST PLACES IN WYOMING TO HAVE BATHTUBS AND ELECTRIC LIGHTS! AND BACK IN THE EARLY 1900S, A LOCAL LEGEND NAMED HOT TAMALE LOUIE SOLD TAMALES AND HAMBURGERS THAT BECAME THE TALK OF THE TOWN.

IN LARAMIE TOWN, THE COWBOYS CHEER,
"GO POKES!" RINGS LOUD FOR ALL TO HEAR.
PISTOL PETE TIPS HIS HAT WITH PRIDE.
HERE, LEARNING AND SPIRIT RIDE SIDE BY SIDE!

GO POKES!

LARAMIE IS HOME TO THE UNIVERSITY OF WYOMING, THE STATE'S ONLY FOUR-YEAR UNIVERSITY! ITS MASCOT, PISTOL PETE, HONORS WYOMING'S COWBOY ROOTS, AND FANS LOVE TO SHOUT "GO POKES!" AT GAMES. THE CAMPUS SITS HIGH ON THE PLAINS, WHERE STUDENTS STUDY BENEATH WIDE BLUE SKIES.

WHY WYOMING? NOW YOU KNOW,
FROM GEYSERS HIGH TO VALLEYS LOW.
A LAND OF BEAUTY, CALM AND TRUE,
WYOMING ALWAYS WELCOMES YOU.

THE END

DEAR READER,

I'VE LIVED IN MANY PLACES ACROSS THE UNITED STATES, BUT THE MOMENT I CAME TO WYOMING, I KNEW I HAD FOUND HOME. THE WIDE-OPEN SKIES, RUGGED MOUNTAINS, AND RICH HISTORY INSPIRED ME TO WRITE THIS BOOK SO I COULD SHARE THE WONDER OF WYOMING WITH OTHERS.

Robin

PS: THERE ARE 24 JACKALOPES HIDING ON THE PAGES OF THIS BOOK, NOT COUNTING THE ONE PLAYING GUITAR. DID YOU FIND THEM ALL?